The Very Important Christmas Pageant

Dennis Hartin

Abingdon Press

Nashville

THE VERY IMPORTANT CHRISTMAS PAGEANT

Copyright © 2006 by Abingdon Press

This book is printed on recycled, acid-free paper.

Scripture quotations in this publication are from the New Revised Standard Version of the Bible, copyright © 1989 by the Division of Christian Education of the National Council of the Churches of Christ in the USA.

ISBN 0-687-33331-8

06 07 08 09 10 11 12 13 14 15 — 10 9 8 7 6 5 4 3 2 1

MANUFACTURED IN THE UNITED STATES OF AMERICA

Contents

Music

Introduction and Production Notes

This pageant is designed for a production with no set, no budget, and no live musical accompaniment. If you have a set, budget, and/or musical accompaniment, you can perform this pageant, too, but you'll have to be really careful, as we'll explain later. Cast members (and production staff) should be dressed to approximate shepherds, wise people, angel, and Bethlehem folk, scrounging up costumes and props. This script comes from the perspective that any attempt by poor, ornery people (like you and like me) to tell the story of God's grace can only be a poor shadow of the glory and mystery of God, no matter what kind of budget or special effects are employed. With that in mind, approach the task as simply as possible, asking for God's grace, and expecting to be surprised.

Why We Go for Laughs

Voltaire said, "God is a comedian playing to an audience too afraid to laugh." Garrison Keillor said, "God writes comedy, it's just that he's stuck with actors who don't know how to play for laughs."

In the classic sense, the Christmas story is the final act of a comedy. By comedy, I mean a story in which two characters try to establish a relationship, then through a series of misadventures, the relationship is endangered but is ultimately established. Every romantic comedy has this structure, as do Shakespeare's comedies. In the Christmas story, the misadventure arises from our inability to accept God's grace, in part because of our expectations.

We're expecting a king riding a chariot, with all the forces of heaven behind. We're getting a baby? OK, then it's a baby born in splendor, right? No, it's a baby born to an unwed mother. In a manger. OK, then, lets have the nation rejoice. Sorry, all you get are shepherds and some Magi from out of town.

Throughout the story, our expectations are dashed—but those are just our expectations. Throughout his narrative, Matthew cites Scripture to show that this topsy-turvy arrangement is what God had in mind all along. You say you don't have those expectations? You say you thought it would be the manger scene all along? I don't believe you. We all expect God to go for the spectacle, because we think God has to impress us to make points. It could be that we think we have to impress God to make points, and we expect God to be like us. I suspect you have those expectations because you've heard the story a thousand times. As a result, you have stopped listening to the story. The absurdity of God's grace should jangle against the ear, which makes it more of a miracle. I am fortunate to have Jewish friends with whom I can talk about my faith, and they never fail to be confounded by the obvious incongruity of the Incarnation. Christians should be confounded by it too.

This pageant looks at the Christmas story from the point of view of the recipients of God's grace as they react with varying degrees of fear, awe, misunderstanding, and hostility.

Production Suggestions

Avoid auditions. A Christmas pageant is not a talent show. The last thing you want is competition. Cast performers with the advice of your assistant directors, or talk to Sunday school teachers before the first rehearsals about who might want to be in the pageant. If there are people you really want in the pageant, ask them. Ask everybody, in fact, and ask them in person.

Hold your scripts. During the pageant, the performers should hold their scripts and speak into microphones on stands. The reproducible script pages are designed to make this easy to accomplish. If you're one of the minority of directors with a pool of performers who memorize well and speak audibly in a large room, or a budget big enough for wireless mikes, ignore the previous sentence. For the rest of us, being on stage produces enough anxiety that holding a script in front of us allows us to relax and enjoy the production. If the idea of seeing all those scripts during the pageant drives you nuts, hide them in hand-held props, such as scrolls or baskets. Remind the cast that the script they are holding is the net, not the trapeze. They must look up when they are speaking. It is very important that the performers speak into the microphones so that the audience can hear the lines.

Look like a pageant. All adults, including ushers, should dress for the event as shepherds, angels, or wise people. It will make it less obvious when an assistant director has to sneak onstage to give a cue or pick something up. At least as important, dressing the adults give the cast the sense that everyone is in this together.

How to Run a Survivable Rehearsal

This pageant is written in three acts, with a prologue and an epilogue. With the possible exception of the Narrators, no cast member appears in more than one act. Everyone is in the prologue and the epilogue. **This makes it possible to rehearse all three acts simultaneously.** The reason for this becomes clear when you recall the typical Christmas pageant rehearsal. This pageant does, however, require that two performers (Herod and Wise Person 3) rehearse the mirror bit in Act Three prior to rehearsals with the rest of the cast (see Script Notes).

Imagine a traditional, three-section, forty-five-minute (including music) pageant script, with Joseph and Mary featured up to the arrival at the inn, then the scene with the shepherds, then the wise people. There may be dialogue between a shepherd and Mary, or the wise people may have a scene with Joseph. Every so often, the group breaks into song. This scenario requires every performer to be available for every part of the rehearsal, with a lot of downtime during rehearsal. Downtime often means kids disrupting the rehearsal or wandering around the church building.

I solved this problem by writing the pageant so that all three acts could be rehearsed simultaneously. With the three acts rehearsed in this way, it is best to have separate narrators for each act, in addition to Narrator 1 and Narrator 2. If a production is shorthanded, Narrator 1 and Narrator 2 could each double "Act One Narrator," "Act Two Narrator," and "Act Three Narrator." That is, Narrator 1 could narrate Act One, Narrator 2 could narrate Act Two, and someone else could narrate Act Three. These suggestions can be adapted as needed based on your unique situation.

An Example of How It Works

First, the director should plan all the blocking for the characters. Using a simple system of X's and O's for each of the characters, draw a blocking chart for each act of the pageant. Keep the blocking simple, focusing especially on getting people on and off the stage without traffic jams. Make copies of the blocking chart for assistant directors.

Second, hold a meeting with at least three assistant directors a few days before the first rehearsal. If there are more than three people who want to help, put someone in charge of finding props and setting them up where they are needed, and put another helper in charge of finding and/or approving costumes. Each assistant director is responsible for rehearsing one act of the pageant. Read through the script and give each director the blocking for the act he or she will direct. Discuss technical issues, such as where microphones will be placed, where the cast will rehearse, who will handle lighting and sound, and so on.

1. At the first rehearsal, everyone assembles in the sanctuary, and the director and assistants gather names. The music director spends ten minutes or so teaching the cast any song that the entire casts needs to know, such as the opening and closing number.

2. At the same time, the director meets in the back of the sanctuary to make casting decisions with the assistant directors, based on who is present. When the music director is finished, the names of the cast are read, along with the name of the assistant director who will rehearse each group.

3. The assistant directors for Act Two and Act Three find separate locations in the church building to hand out scripts and to rehearse blocking and lines. The director begins the rehearsal with the Act One cast, going through blocking and lines.

4. After twenty-five minutes, the assistant director for Act Two brings his or her group back to the sanctuary. The Act One cast leaves with their assistant director and reviews their blocking and lines in another part of the church.

5. Twenty-five minutes later, the assistant director for Act Three brings his or her group to the sanctuary. The Act Two group leaves the sanctuary to review what they have done.

Instead of rehearsing a forty-five-minute pageant in which each cast member spends most of the time waiting to rehearse, have three rehearsals of three short scenes, in which each cast member has work to do nearly all the time. Cast members have less time to get bored and into mischief and they are more comfortable during the performance, since they have spent more time actually rehearsing.

The music director assigns and rehearses the music separately from the rest of the production weeks before the two rehearsals described here. The people performing the music should not also be part of the dramatic cast in the three acts, to ensure that each part of the pageant can be rehearsed separately. If the rotating sessions in the sanctuary go well, add a quick run-through at the end of the first two-hour rehearsal. Alternately, the director can go from room to room as the three acts rehearse.

	10 Minutes	25 Minutes	25 Minutes	25 Minutes	35 Minutes
Sanctuary	ALL	Act One	Act Two	Act Three	ALL (run-through)
Room A		Act Two	Act One	Act One	
Room B		Act Three	Act Three	Act Two	

The timeline shows a possible two-hour rehearsal, including where each group meets and the duration of each rehearsal. If your cast will be memorizing the script, use the same model and add more rehearsals, as needed. If you need more time for one act, appropriate five minutes from the act rehearsing in the sanctuary and five minutes from the run-through time to focus attention on the act that needs more work.

The second rehearsal is a straight run-through with music. Remember to watch the clock, and to skip over parts that are already well rehearsed. Make sure that all cast members know when they have an entrance. Since the cast will be holding scripts, the director's main job is traffic control. As much as is possible, place an assistant wherever a character will make an entrance. An assistant can sit with the wise people and the angel to cue them when to speak or when to enter.

Musical Notes

- **Don't have the congregation sing.** This allows you to keep the lights over the congregation low, and gives them the sense that they are at an "event," rather than a service of worship.

- **Don't do the old standbys, unless you can find new ways to present them.** The music suggestions and the enclosed CD offer you a few new songs and a few familiar songs to sing in a new way. The one exception to this rule: The children in second grade and younger always have an ensemble title and sing "Away in a Manger." There are two reasons for this: (1) Parents really like it. If they're put off by anything else in the pageant, we can get forgiveness by having the little ones sing; and (2) I like it!

About This Edition

The package you hold in your hands is designed so that any church can produce a pageant. If you don't have a live accompanist, you can play the enclosed CD accompaniment for the songs. If you do have an accompanist, use the CD for the sound effects. You can also use music that is not included here if you prefer.

This pageant is not about you. Or your church. Or even the kids in your church. It is about God's grace among us and our reaction to that grace. One way we confound God's grace is by taking ourselves too seriously—that was certainly Herod's problem. Resist the temptation to do something with or to the script just to show how clever or talented you (or the performers) are. Resist the urge to punch up the script to get bigger laughs. In comedy, as in life, bigger is not always better. Resist the urge to add production values simply for the sake of looking more dramatic or professional. There is nothing quite so lame as trying to recreate the grandeur of God through our little human efforts, no matter how big a budget you can muster. Ask yourself this question as often as you need to: "Are we doing this because we are trying to make God's grace more apparent to the audience, or are we just trying to show off how clever and talented we are?"

Whatever you do, you should do as well as you can, secure in God's grace. Speaking of grace, I should include a word about "flubs." Nearly every "cute" pageant story is about some kid muffing a line or missing an entrance. Allow your performers the chance for memorable moments of excellence, rather than having their miscues tell the story. Show them that you respect them, as well as the story being told.

The Nativity is a story of people who don't know how to act in the light of God's grace. We are these people. This is a children's story, not just because we associate Christmas with children, but because they are a perfect vehicle for material showing equal parts trepidation and boldness in the face of circumstances both comforting and challenging. That is the nature of theater and the nature of the gospel. This pageant is intended as a re-creation, not just a retelling, of the Nativity story. It is the task of the directors, actors, musicians, and all to proclaim God's grace and expect a response. The response, of course, comes from the audience. It is a simple story. Stay out of its way.

Author's Note

According to Luke, when the disciples were having a disputation about which of them was the greatest, Jesus put an end to the conversation by means of a nearby visual aide. He stood by a small child and said, "Whoever welcomes this child in my name welcomes me, and whoever welcomes me, welcomes the one who sent me, for the least among all of you is the greatest" (Luke 9:48).

I don't recall ever having a conversation in a group where people were explicitly asking the question, "Which of us is the greatest?" I have, however, been in and been privy to many conversations in which the conversation was about the relative greatness of the participants. In those conversations, the topic was not the participants themselves, it was their education or their possessions, their attitudes or their insight, or something they had or something they did that made them important—at least as important as anyone there, and maybe more important than everyone there.

Into the midst of a discussion like this, Jesus walks in with a child and says, "You want important? I'll give you important." Welcome a child on my behalf, and you're welcoming God. This seems like an indirect way of welcoming God, but God has an indirect way of welcoming us—just look at the Christmas story.

In the Nativity, God puts aside our notions of what makes us important—indeed, he kicks over what we think makes God important—to introduce us to a child that we should welcome. It seems a very unimportant thing, the birth of this baby, but the angels of Heaven cannot contain their joy, and Herod cannot contain his fear.

Had we been in charge of the assignment of proclaiming God's grace to the world, we would have gone straight to the top, shaken our finger at Herod, and admonished him to bow down to the new ruler who was about to enter flanked by charioteers and infantry. Of course, that assumes that the new ruler was entering flanked by charioteers and infantry, which we would have insisted on, since we were in charge.

But, we weren't in charge. And rather than proclaim the Good News to the high and mighty, God takes ordinary people and tells them that the Extraordinary is among them. It seems almost an afterthought that word about the Word gets out: Herod finds out almost in passing from a group of people wise enough to know they don't know what's going on; and we never hear what the shepherds say after visiting the stable.

But the word is out: welcoming a child is how you welcome God.

Cast List

Prologue/Epilogue
- Narrator 1 (Reporter)
- Narrator 2 (Angel)

Act One
- Act One Narrator
- Mary
- Angel
- Joseph
- Desk Clerk

Act Two
- Act Two Narrator
- Shepherd 1
- Shepherd 2
- Angel
- Haste (Shepherd)
- Various Shepherds
- Various Angels

Act Three
- Act Three Narrator
- Major Domo
- Herod
- Wise Person 1
- Wise Person 2
- Wise Person 3
- Wise Person 4
- Voices Off (2)

Prop and Costume List

This is a list of props necessary to perform the script that follows. It is not an exhaustive list of everything you may want to use. For instance, you could give rough-hewn crooks to some of the shepherds so that they look a little more like shepherds. Costumes are always a fun addition. Remember that the cast may be holding their scripts as they perform, so trying to juggle a script and extra props may be more than your cast will be able to do.

PROPS

Prologue

• Flash camera

Act One

• Little table

Act Two

• Hotel Bell

• "No Pets" sign

Act Three

• Junk for shepherd music

COSTUMES

Simple, biblical costumes are appropriate for most of the cast. The basic costume is an oversized long-sleeve tunic that is usually worn with a fabric belt or cord. Head coverings can be made by folding a square of cloth diagonally with the fold across the forehead and a cord tied around the head to hold the head covering in place. Sandals are worn by both men and women. Adapt the costume based on the character.

Narrators and Major Domo wear simple, calf-length tunics in solid colors, and plain sandals. The Shepherds wear undyed, natural fabrics, such as muslin or linen. The Angel's tunic should be white and ankle-length. Mary's robe is traditionally in blue. Joseph wears a long tunic and a cloak in plain neutral-colored fabric. The Wise People would be dressed in finer fabrics in rich colors, such as purple, red, or royal blue, with elaborate head coverings and jewelry. Herod would wear a long robe with a cloak, a crown, large rings, and other elaborate jewelry. All other cast members can wear plain tunics or robes with simple fabric head coverings and sandals.

Prologue

1
2　　 **"Overture: Love Came Down at Christmas"**
3　　(CD #1, *Instrumental*)
4
5 **Narrator 1:** Good evening. On behalf of *(insert committee or church*
6　　*school name)* and in the name of our Lord Jesus Christ, welcome to
7　　the *(your church name here)* Church Christmas Pageant!
8　　　I would like to record this joyous moment for posterity *(takes out*
9　　*camera)*, so would you all please say, "Christmas!" You folks on the
10　　outside of the pews, could you lean in a little?
11　　　OK—"Christmas!" *(Takes picture.)* Very good. And one more, just
12　　in case. *(Takes another picture.)*
13　　　The good news is, we have this joyous moment recorded for
14　　posterity. The bad news is, you all now have blue dots floating in
15　　front of your eyes. If you take pictures during the pageant, that's
16　　what will happen to the people up here. They will be moving
17　　around and reading scripts, so the flashes could distract them and
18　　could be dangerous. We also need the aisles clear, so please don't
19　　do any videotaping, either. After the pageant, you can create all the
20　　floating blue dots you want. Thank you.
21　　　Tonight, we have a rare opportunity to go behind the scene of
22　　the Christmas story. Standing with me is a real live angel.
23
24 **Narrator 2:** *(Dressed as an angel)* Good evening. I am Archangel
25　　Harold, Squadron Leader for the 25th Airborne Division of the
26　　Heavenly Host.
27
28 **Narrator 1:** Hark, you're Harold Angel?
29
30 **Narrator 2:** That's right. *(Pause)* What's the matter?
31
32 **Narrator 1:** I thought that was a song cue.
33
34 **Narrator 2:** Sorry, no.

35 **Narrator 1:** As an angel, you've had some really tough assignments,
36   haven't you?
37
38 **Narrator 2:** That's right. As you know, the task of an angel is to carry
39   messages of God to the people of God. In our time, we've delivered
40   messages of plagues, pestilence, and all kinds of awful stuff.
41
42 **Narrator 1:** But tonight, you'll be delivering your most important
43   message, is that right?
44
45 **Narrator 2:** That's right.
46
47 **Narrator 1:** Tell me, what could be more important than messages of
48   plagues, pestilence, and all sorts of other awful stuff?
49
50 **Narrator 2:** Birth announcements.
51
52 **Narrator 1:** Excuse me?
53
54 **Narrator 2:** Birth announcements. We will be delivering the news of the
55   birth of the Messiah, who will redeem his people and be the living
56   proof of God's love to all generations.
57
58 **Narrator 1:** And who will receive these birth announcements? Kings?
59   Potentates? Prime Ministers?
60
61 **Narrator 2:** Actually, we will deliver the announcements to a teenage
62   girl in Nazareth and a bunch of shepherds.
63
64 **Narrator 1:** Excuse me? You're telling me that the news of the most
65   important birth in the history of the world will be brought first to
66   some kid in a backwater town and some wool wranglers?
67
68 **Narrator 2:** That's about the way it looks. Now, if you'll excuse me,
69   we've got to get some angels airborne, and you're standing in the
70   middle of the flight line.
71
72   **"Love Came Down At Christmas"** (CD #2)
73

Act One

1 **Act One Narrator:** In the sixth month the angel Gabriel was sent from
2   God to a city of Galilee named Nazareth, to a virgin betrothed to a
3   man whose name was Joseph, of the house of David; and the
4   virgin's name was Mary. And he came to her and said, "Hail, O
5   favored one, the Lord is with you!" But she was greatly troubled at
6   the saying, and considered in her mind what sort of greeting this
7   might be. And the angel said to her, "Do not be afraid Mary, for you
8   have found favor with God. And behold, you will conceive in your
9   womb and bear a son, and you shall call his name Jesus." And
10 Mary said to the angel, "How can this be, since I have no
11 husband?" And the angel said to her, "He will be great and will be
12 called the Son of the Most High, and the Lord God will give to him
13 the throne of his father David, and he will reign over the house of
14 Jacob forever and of his kingdom there will be no end."

15
16 *(**Angel** does fake door knock. **Mary** answers.)*
17
18 **Mary:** Yes?
19
20 **Angel:** Is this the home of Mary, the betrothed of Joseph?
21
22 **Mary:** Yes, it is, but we don't accept door-to-door solicitations—
23
24 **Angel:** But that's not why I'm—
25
26 **Mary:** So please put us on your "Do Not Call" list.
27
28 **Angel:** Hail, O Favored One! The Lord is with you!
29
30 **Mary:** I'm sure he is. Have a nice day.
31
32 **Angel:** Please don't shut the door. I'm here to deliver a message.
33
34 **Mary:** The mailman wears a blue uniform.

35 **Angel:** I don't work for the Postal Service.

36

37 **Mary:** Then, who do you work for?

38

39 **Angel:** Look at the wings. What do they mean?

40

41 **Mary:** You work for the Philadelphia Eagles? *(See Script Notes.)*

42

43 **Angel:** No, no. I'm an angel.

44

45 **Mary:** Yeah, right. And I'm a pop star. *(See Script Notes.)*

46

47 **Angel:** Just hear me out. I have a message for you, from God.

48

49 **Mary:** You know, you're not making this any easier for yourself.

50

51 **Angel:** Why is it so hard for you to believe I'm an angel?

52

53 **Mary:** Assuming, just assuming you're for real—take a look around.
54   You're in a house with a dirt floor and no windows. Why would an
55   angel visit a nobody like me?

56

57 **Angel:** There are no "nobodies." You are very important.

58

59 **Mary:** To whom?

60

61 **Angel:** God.

62

63 **Mary:** God made the stars and the earth and the oceans. Those are
64   important.

65

66 **Angel:** You are made of exactly the same stuff as the stars and the
67   earth and the oceans. You are important.

68

69 **Mary:** So, what's the message?

70

71 **Angel:** Do not be afraid, Mary, for you have found favor with God. And
72   behold, you will conceive in your womb and bear a son, and you
73   shall call his name Jesus. He will be great and will be called the

74	Son of the Most High, and the Lord God will give to him the throne
75	of his father David, and he will reign over the house of Jacob
76	forever and of his kingdom there will be no end.
77	
78	**Mary:** How can this be, if I have no husband?
79	
80	**Angel:** The Holy Spirit will come upon you, and the power of the Most
81	High will overshadow you; therefore the child to be born of you will
82	be called holy, the Son of God.
83	
84	**Mary:** That's quite a message.
85	
86	**Angel:** You seem scared.
87	
88	**Mary:** I am. But I am the handmaid of the Lord. Let it be according to
89	your word.
90	
91	♫ **"The Angel Spoke to Young Mary"** (CD #3)
92	
93	**Act One Narrator:** In those days a decree went out from Caesar
94	Augustus that all the world should be enrolled. This was the first
95	enrollment, when Quirinius was governor of Syria. And all went to be
96	enrolled, each to his own city.
97	
98	**Joseph:** Mary, it's me!
99	
100	**Mary:** Joseph! I have the most amazing news!
101	
102	**Joseph:** What a coincidence! I have amazing news, too.
103	
104	**Mary:** Well, mine is very amazing!
105	
106	**Joseph:** Well, I think mine is even more amazing!
107	
108	**Mary:** Oh, you do, do you? Tell me your amazing news.
109	
110	**Joseph:** I just heard that a decree has gone forth from Caesar Augustus
111	that all the world should be enrolled!
112	

113   **Mary:** We're going to be enrolled?

114

115   **Joseph:** Right!

116

117   **Mary:** Enrolled in what? I haven't finished high school yet.

118

119   **Joseph:** No, no. Enrolled with the Emperor, so he can raise taxes.

120

121   **Mary:** That's the amazing news?

123

124   **Joseph:** Mary, for this enrollment, everyone has to go to their own city.

125

126   **Mary:** So?

127

128   **Joseph:** So, in a few months, everyone's going to pack up their
129   possessions and haul them all over the country.

130

131   **Mary:** I'm listening.

132

133   **Joseph:** They're going to need carts!

134

135   **Mary:** But you're a carpenter, not a cartwright!

136

137   **Joseph:** No problem. See this table? Flip it over, put on a couple of
138   wheels and a handle—it's a cart. If I put in some overtime, I
139   could have a gross of these done before everybody hits the road.
140   Mary, this could be just the beginning—I could go from being an
141   unimportant carpenter to a transportation king! How was your
142   day?

143

144   **Mary:** An angel appeared to me and said that the Holy Spirit will come
145   upon me and I will carry a child who will be the Son of the Most
146   High and that God will give him the throne of David.

147

148   **Joseph:** *(Pause)* OK, you win. That's much more amazing than my
149   news.

150

151   **"It Came Upon the Midnight Clear"** (CD #4)

152

153 **Act One Narrator:** And Joseph also went up from Galilee, from the city
154   of Nazareth, to Judea, to the city of David, which is called Bethlehem,
155   because he was of the house and lineage of David, to be enrolled with
156   Mary, his betrothed, who was with child. And while they were there,
157   the time came for her to be delivered. And she gave birth to her
158   firstborn son and wrapped him in swaddling cloths, and laid him in a
159   manger, because there was no room for them in the inn.
160
161 (**Joseph** taps the Hotel Bell.)
162
163   **SFX:** *Hotel Desk Bell* (CD #5)
164
165 **Desk Clerk:** May I help you?
166
167 **Joseph:** Yes, I have a reservation.
168
169 **Desk Clerk:** Name?
170
171 **Joseph:** Joseph.
172
173 **Desk Clerk:** Let me see . . . Joseph Cartwright?
174
175 **Joseph:** No, I'm a carpenter.
176
177 **Desk Clerk:** All right, here we . . . oh, I'm sorry, but we had to cancel
178   your reservation.
179
180 **Joseph:** What?
181
182 **Desk Clerk:** Well, with the enrollment and all, there are a lot of important
183   people converging on Bethlehem. And all these important people
184   travel with huge entourages. And, as you know, Bethlehem is a
185   little town.
186
187 **Joseph:** I know.
188
189 **Desk Clerk:** (*Pause*) Is something wrong?
190
191 **Joseph:** I thought that was a song cue.

192 **Desk Clerk:** Sorry, no.

193

194 **Joseph:** So, what am I supposed to do? My wife's going to have a baby
195   any minute, I have a donkey pulling a cart full of stuff—

196

197 **Desk Clerk:** Where?

198

199 **Joseph:** Out there.

200

201 **Desk Clerk:** That's a cart? Looks like somebody just jammed some
202   wheels and a handle on a table. Hope you didn't pay much for it.

203

204 **Joseph:** Can we get back to my reservation?

205

206 **Desk Clerk:** I'm sorry about that, but there's no room at the inn. But,
207   given your circumstances, I think we can accommodate you.

208

209 **Joseph:** Really?

210

211 **Desk Clerk:** Sure. There's room in the stable.

212

213 **Joseph:** The stable? What kind of place is that for my wife to have a—

214

215 **Desk Clerk:** I realize it's not your first choice. But, think for a moment:
216   in his first moments of life, your child will be surrounded by the
217   kindest of God's creatures. Contented cows. Loyal horses. Playful
218   goats. Gentle sheep. What a joy it will be for him to be surrounded
219   by these pure spirits.

220

221 **Joseph:** I hadn't thought of that. OK, we'll take the stable. Is there room
222   in there for me to keep my donkey?

223

224 **Desk Clerk:** Yes, there's room, but your donkey will have to stay on the
225   street.

226

227 **Joseph:** How come?

228

229 **Desk Clerk:** *(Holds up "No Pets" sign and reads.)* No Pets!

Act Two

1
2 🎵 **"O Little Town Of Bethlehem"** (CD #6)
3
4 **Act Two Narrator:** And in that region there were shepherds out in the
5 field, keeping watch over their flock by night. And an angel of the
6 Lord appeared to them, and the glory of the Lord shone around them
7 and they were filled with fear. And the angel said to them, "Be not
8 afraid, for behold, I bring you good news of a great joy which will
9 come to all the people; for to you is born this day in the city of David
10 a Savior, who is Christ the Lord. And this will be a sign for you: you
11 will find a babe wrapped in swaddling cloths and lying in a manger."
12 And suddenly there was with the angel a multitude of the heavenly
13 host praising God and saying, "Glory to God in the highest, and on
14 earth, peace, good will to all." When the angels went away to heaven,
15 the shepherds said to one another, "Let us go over to Bethlehem and
16 see this thing that has happened and which the Lord has made
17 known to us." And they went with haste, and found Mary and
18 Joseph, and the babe lying in a manger. And when they saw it they
19 made known the saying which had been told them concerning this
20 child; and all who heard it wondered at what the shepherds told
21 them. But Mary kept all these things, pondering them in her heart.
22 And the shepherds returned, glorifying and praising God for all they
23 had heard and seen, as it had been told them.
24
25 (**Shepherds** enter the stage area, which is festooned with junk. One
26 shepherd, **Haste**, is uninvolved, and goes off to a corner to sleep.)
27
28 **Shepherd 1:** Look at all this garbage!
29
30 **Shepherd 2:** Yeah, look at all this!
31
32 **Shepherd 1:** This hillside is a mess!
33
34 **Shepherd 2:** What a mess!

35 **Shepherd 1:** Our sheep can't safely graze here!
36
37 **Shepherd 2:** No they can't!
38
39 **Shepherd 1:** What kind of pigs would do this?
40
41 **Shepherd 2:** Pigs!
42
43 **Shepherd 1:** Why do you repeat everything I say?
44
45 **Shepherd 2:** Do I repeat everything you say?
46
47 **Shepherd 1:** I just said, "What pigs?" and you said—
48
49 **Shepherd 2:** Pigs!
50
51 **Shepherd 1:** That's what I mean, I said—
52
53 **Shepherd 2:** Pigs!
54
55 **Shepherd 1:** and you said—
56
57 **Shepherd 2:** Pigs!
58
59 **Shepherd 1:** I just want to know who did this!
60
61 **Shepherd 2:** Pigs! Real pigs! The swineherds were on this hill last
62   night!
63
64 **Shepherd 1:** Oh. That explains it. OK, guys, let's pick all this up!
65
66   (**Shepherds** *start picking up garbage.*)
67
68   **"O Come, O Come, Emmanuel"** (CD #7, *Junk Band*)
69
70 **Shepherd 1:** OK, guys, that was real pretty. Know any other tunes?
71
72   (*Herald trumpets from balcony.*)

73
74   **SFX**: *Herald Trumpet* (CD #8)

75

76 **Shepherd 1:** Nice tune, but a little short—

77

78 **Shepherd 2:** Uh, chief?

79

80 **Shepherd 1:** We're going to be here all night, maybe you could—

81

82 **Shepherd 2:** Chief?

83

84 **Shepherd 1:** —expand your repertoire. What?

85

86 **Shepherd 2:** The music didn't come from us.

87

88 **Shepherd 1:** Then where did it come from?

89

90 **Shepherd 2:** *(Pointing to balcony.)* Up there.

91

92 **Shepherd 1:** Up where? We're on top of a hill, junior. There isn't
93   anything up there but— whoa!

94

95 **Angel:** Be not afraid!

96

97 **Shepherd 2:** Give me one good reason why.

98

99 **Angel:** For behold, I bring you good news of great joy which will come
100   to all the people; for to you is born this day in the city of David a
101   Savior, who is Christ the Lord.

102

103   (**Shepherds** *ad lib astonishment.*)

104

105 **Shepherd 1:** Hold it! Hold it! Excuse me, big person with wings.
106   Meaning no disrespect, but are you sure you're hovering over the
107   right hillside? I mean, you're proclaiming the birth of God's grace
108   incarnate to a crowd of ragtag, illiterate shepherds.

109

110 **Angel:** Don't sell yourself short. You have remarkable musical talent.

111   **Shepherd 1:** Well, thanks, but that hardly explains—
112
113   **Angel:** You have taken things that were thought to be of no importance
114   and made something wonderful from them. This night, God is
115   doing the same. And this will be a sign for you: you will find the
116   babe wrapped in swaddling clothes, lying in a manger.
117
118   **Angel Chorus:** Glory to God in the highest, and on earth peace, good
119   will among all!
120
121   **Shepherd 2:** Let us go over to Bethlehem and see this thing that has
122   happened and which the Lord has made known to us! *(Ad lib*
123   *commotion.)*
124
125   **Shepherd 1:** Whoa, whoa! If we're going to go, let's go with Haste!
126
127   **Shepherd 2:** We're going with Haste?
128
129   **Shepherd 1:** Sure thing. Hey, Haste!
130
131   **Haste:** *(Waking up quickly)* Yeah, boss?
132
133   **Shepherd 1:** Shake a leg! We're going to a baby shower!
134
135   **"Away In A Manger"** (CD #9)

Act Three

1   **Act Three Narrator:** Now when Jesus was born in Bethlehem of Judea in
2   the days of Herod the king, behold, wise people from the East came to
3   Jerusalem, saying, "Where is he who is born king of the Jews? For we
4   have seen his star in the East, and have come to worship him." Herod
5   summoned the wise men secretly and ascertained from them what
6   time the star appeared and he sent them to Bethlehem saying, "Go
7   and search diligently for the child, and when you have found him
8   bring me word, that I too may come and worship him."
9

10   **Major Domo:** Good day, King Herod.
11

12   **Herod:** You're absolutely right it's a good day! And you know why it's a
13   good day?
14

15   **Major Domo:** Well, I—
16

17   **Herod:** Because I'm king, that's why! Because I'm the greatest king of
18   all. And if it's not a good day for me, it's not a good day for
19   anybody! Get it?
20

21   **Major Domo:** Got it.
22

23   **Herod:** Good.
24

25   **Major Domo:** I have your schedule for the day. You will begin with the
26   "Herod Appreciation Week" kick-off breakfast.
27

28   **Herod:** I thought we had "Herod Appreciation Week" last week.
29

30   **Major Domo:** No, last week was "Herod Recognition Week."
31

32   **Herod:** I thought that was next week.
33

34   **Major Domo:** No, next week is "Herod's a Jolly Good Fellow Week."

35   **Herod:** That's my favorite.

36

37   **Major Domo:** Anyway, the kick-off breakfast is in the auxiliary dining hall.

38

39   **Herod:** How come we're not doing it here in the Grand Hall?

40

41   **Major Domo:** Because we're closing the Grand Hall today. Workmen are
42   coming to install that large mirror you wanted over there. *(Points to*
43   *future location of mirror.)*

44

45   **Herod:** Wonderful. When that mirror is installed, I will be able to see my
46   own exalted reflection from every spot in the palace. What's next?

47

48   **Major Domo:** We're expecting a delegation of wise people from the east
49   to arrive sometime today.

50

51   **Herod:** Wise people? What do they want?

52

53   **Major Domo:** According to their advance man, they're coming to give
54   gifts and offer praises to the king.

55

56   **Herod:** Boy, I love this job.

57

58   **Major Domo:** Your highness, we're late for the breakfast. We'd better be
59   going.

60

61   **Herod:** You go on ahead. I'll be in the Royal Washroom. Not that I need to
62   wash up, I just like the look of solid gold faucets. (**Major Domo** *and*
63   **Herod** *exit opposite ways.* **Wise People** *enter from rear, cautiously.)*

64

65   ♫ **"The First Noel"** (CD #10)

66

67   **Wise Person 1:** Hello? Anyone here?

68

69   **Wise Person 2:** Are you sure we're in the right palace?

70

71   **Wise Person 3:** I'm sure. Look at the size of this place!

72

73   **Wise Person 4:** I'll bet even the closets have closets!

74 **Wise Person 2:** This doesn't seem like a good idea to me.
75

76 **Wise Person 1:** We'll find someone who knows something about a king
77 being born, get directions and we'll be on our way.
78

79 **Wise Person 3:** I thought we were following the star.
80

81 **Wise Person 1:** The star? Did you see where the star was headed? It
82 was leading us downtown. To the industrial district. Nothing there
83 but low rent apartments and crummy inns. Believe me, if there's a
84 king being born there, it's no king like I've ever seen.
85

86 **Wise Person 2:** Let's find a butler or a footman. Where is everybody?
87

88 **Wise Person 3:** But, the star is the sign—
89

90 *(Herald trumpets)*
91

92 **SFX:** *Herald Trumpet* (CD #11)
93

94 **Voice Off:** Make way for King Herod!
95

96 **Wise Person 1:** The king?
96

98 **Wise Person 3:** We haven't been announced! He'll think we're burglars!
99

100 **Wise Person 1:** Scatter!
101

102 *(**Wise People** scatter, except for **Wise Person 3**, who is caught onstage*
103 *as **Herod** enters. **Wise Person 3** is standing right where the mirror is*
104 *supposed to be installed. They perform the Mirror Bit.) (See Script*
105 *Notes, page 32.)*
106

107 **Major Domo:** *(Entering offstage)* Oh, mighty king!
108

109 *(**Herod** turns at **Major Domo's** voice. **Wise Person 3** bolts before*
110 ***Herod** or **Major Domo** sees him.)*
111

112 **Herod:** What?

113 **Major Domo:** *(Enters.)* You missed breakfast.
114
115 **Herod:** I was busy admiring myself in the new mirror.
116
117 **Major Domo:** What mirror?
118
119 **Herod:** The one right— *(He is momentarily baffled that there is no*
120   *mirror.)* So, when's lunch?
121
122 **Major Domo:** Shortly. But first, we have some guests. I met them as
123   they were wandering the halls. Mighty King Herod, may I introduce
124   the wise people from the East!
125
126 **Herod:** *(Looking at **Wise Person 3** closely)* Have we met?
127
128 **Wise Person 3:** No, no, no, no, no. No. *(**Wise Person 3** quickly puts on*
129   *sunglasses.)*
130
131 **Herod:** My mistake. Anyway, let me welcome you to the magnificent
132   Herod's Palace. I am, of course, the magnificent Herod. It is my
133   pleasure to meet you all, and please extend my best wishes to your
134   country when you return home.
135
136 **Wise Person 1:** Mighty Herod, we are most—
137
138 **Herod:** Skip the small talk, what'd you bring me?
139
140 **Wise Person 2:** Nothing.
141
142 **Herod:** What?
143
144 **Wise Person 1:** What he means is, we have brought presents for a
145   newborn king.
146
147 **Wise Person 3:** We've been following a star.
148
149 **Herod:** A king whose birth is announced with a star?
150
151 **Major Domo:** This could be trouble.

152 **Herod:** Yes, well, um, look, forget about giving me the presents. Just
153   find the newborn king, come back here and let me know where to
154   find him so I may worship him, too.
155
156 **Wise Person 1:** Uh, sure.
157
158 **Herod:** By the way, what are you bringing him?
159
160 **Wise Person 1:** Gold.
161
162 **Wise Person 2:** Frankincense.
163
164 **Wise Person 3:** Myrrh.
165
166 **Wise Person 4:** Pears from Harry and David.
167
168 **Wise Person 1:** We ate those, remember?
169
170 **Herod:** Nice. Well, when I find him—that is, when I worship him, I'll
171   bring him one of these.
172
173 **Wise Person 1:** What is that?
174
175 **Herod:** Herod's Palace Souvenir Key Ring.
176
177 **Wise Person 1:** Nice.
178
179 **Herod:** Glows in the dark.
180
181 **Act Three Narrator:** When they had heard the king they went on their
182   way; and lo, the star which they had seen in the East went before
183   them, till it came to rest over the place where the child was. When
184   they saw the star, they rejoiced exceedingly with great joy; and
185   going into the house they saw the child with Mary his mother, and
186   they fell down and worshiped him.
187
188
189   **"Joy To The World"** (CD #12)

Epilogue

1 **Narrator 1:** Well, there you have it. A fully detailed look at the
2 Christmas story. And, before we go, we're fortunate to have Harold
3 Angel here for a final word.
4
5 **Narrator 2:** Thank you, Biff. Folks, let me remind you that the
6 Christmas story happened to people just like you. Well, maybe a
7 little shorter than you, but basically the same. Every one of those
8 people were important to God—just like you. Remember what the
9 angels sing, "Love came down at Christmas." *(Pause)* Is something
10 wrong?
11
12 **Narrator 1:** I thought that was a song cue.
13
14 **Narrator 2:** Actually, it is.
15
16
17 🎵 **"Love Came Down at Christmas"** (CD #13)

Song Texts

Love Came Down at Christmas
(one stanza version)

1. Love came down at Christmas,
   Love all lovely, Love divine;
   Love was born at Christmas;
   star and angels gave the sign.

The Angel Spoke to Young Mary

1. The angel spoke to young Mary;
   The angel spoke to young Mary;
   The angel spoke to young Mary;
   hallelujah forevermore.

2. Oh Mary, you have found favor;
   Oh Mary, you have found favor;
   Oh Mary, you have found favor;
   hallelujah forevermore.

3. The baby will be called Jesus;
   The baby will be called Jesus;
   The baby will be called Jesus;
   hallelujah forevermore.

It Came upon the Midnight Clear

1. It came upon the midnight clear,
   that glorious song of old,
   from angels bending near the earth,
   to touch their harps of gold:
   "Peace on the earth, good will to
   all, from heaven's all-gracious
   King."
   The world in solemn stillness lay
   to hear the angels sing.

2. Still through the cloven skies they
   come with peaceful wings
   unfurled,
   and still their heavenly music
   floats o'er all the weary world;
   above its sad and lowly plains,
   they bend on hovering wing,
   and ever o'er its Babel sounds the
   blessed angels sing.

O Little Town of Bethlehem

1. O little town of Bethlehem, how
     still we see thee lie;
   above thy deep and dreamless
     sleep the silent stars go by.
   Yet in thy dark streets shineth
     the everlasting light;
   the hopes and fears of all the
     years are met in thee tonight.

2. O holy Child of Bethlehem,
     descend to us, we pray;
   cast out our sin, and enter in,
     be born in us today.
   We hear the Christmas angels
     the great glad tidings tell;
   O come to us, abide with us,
     our Lord Emmanuel!

O Come, O Come, Emmanuel

O come, Desire of nations bind
  all peoples in one heart and mind.
From dust thou brought us
  forth to life;
deliver us from earthly strife.
Rejoice! Rejoice!
Emmanuel shall come to thee,
  O Israel.

Away in a Manger

1. Away in a manger, no crib for a bed,
   the little Lord Jesus laid down his
     sweet head.
   The stars in the sky looked down
     where he lay,
   the little Lord Jesus asleep on the
     hay.

2. The cattle are lowing, the baby
     awakes,
   but little Lord Jesus, no crying he
     makes;
   I love thee, Lord Jesus, look down
     from the sky
   and stay by my cradle till morning
     is nigh.

3. Be near me, Lord Jesus, I ask the
     to stay
   close by me forever, and love me,
     I pray;
   bless all the dear children in thy
     tender care,
   and fit us for heaven to live with
     thee there.

The First Noel

1. The first Noel the angel did say
   was to certain poor shepherds
   in fields as they lay;
   in fields where they lay keeping
   their sheep,
   on a cold winter's night that was
   so deep.
   Noel, Noel, Noel, Noel,
   born is the King of Israel.

2. They looked up and saw a star
   shining in the east, beyond them
   far;
   and to the earth it gave great light,
   and so it continued both day
   and night.
   Noel, Noel, Noel, Noel,
   born is the King of Israel.

3. And by the light of that same star
   the Wise Men came from country
   far;
   to seek for a king was their intent,
   and to follow the star wherever it
   went.
   Noel, Noel, Noel, Noel,
   born is the King of Israel.

Joy to the World

1. Joy to the world, the Lord is come!
   Let earth receive her King;
   let every heart prepare him room,
   and heaven and nature sing,
   and heaven and nature sing,
   and heaven, and heaven, and
   nature sing.

2. He rules the world with truth and
   grace,
   and makes the nations prove
   the glories of his righteousness,
   and wonders of his love,
   and wonders of his love,
   and wonders, wonders of his love.

Love Came Down
at Christmas
(Full Version)

1. Love came down at Christmas,
   Love all lovely, Love divine;
   Love was born was born at
   Christmas;
   star and angel gave the sign,

2. Worship we the Godhead,
   Love incarnate, Love divine;
   worship we our Jesus,
   but wherewith for sacred sign?

3. Love shall be our token;
   love be yours and love be mine;
   love to God and neighbor,
   love for plea and gift and sign.

Script Notes

Act One

★ "the Philadephia Eagles"— If you have a local sports team whose nickname is some kind of bird, you could substitute the name here.

★ "And I'm a pop star"—You may substitute the name of any currently famous film/song/pop culture diva.

★ "That's a cart? It looks like somebody just jammed some wheels and a handle on a table."— Don't feel compelled to actually construct such a contraption. As long as Joseph points offstage when he says, "Out there," and the Innkeeper looks the same direction when he delivers his line, you won't need it.

Act Two
The Junk Band

The CD accompanying this script includes a recording of a junk band version of "O Come, O Come, Emmanuel." You may mime a performance of a junk band along with the recording.

If you're so inclined, though, and have the resources, you may want to have your own junk band. Simply gather a bunch of stuff from your garage, kitchen, and storage shed. Metal pipes, hammers, metal stuff of all kinds, sandpaper to rub together, metal and plastic buckets, broomsticks—anything that makes noise when you slap it or bend it!

Your music person at church can help you develop the patterns for the junk band. Divide the "instruments" into three to four different groups and teach each group a pattern as suggested by the music person. It may be that your cast is talented enough to develop the patterns themselves by listening to the CD! The point is to have fun. If you really get into this you can try www.stomponline.com for listening clips and videos.

Act Three
The Mirror Bit

One character thinks he (or she) is looking into a mirror, when actually he is looking at a second character. Character 2 is determined that Character 1 will continue to think that he is looking in a mirror. Somehow, Character 2 is able to anticipate and reproduce every move Character 1 makes, even when

Character 1 begins to grow suspicious and make moves that are sudden or hard to anticipate.

That is the mirror bit, and it has been around at least since a vaudeville act called the Schwartz Brothers performed it before World War I. It is a tricky bit of business, because it requires at least as much choreography as acting. You'll need two really good performers to accomplish this; you will also need time to rehearse them separately and apart from the rest of the cast. But, if it works, it's worth it. There are two examples of the mirror bit available: (1) a scene from the Marx Brothers' movie *Duck Soup,* and (2) the episode of *I Love Lucy* in which Harpo Marx appeared. Both of these are much more complicated and much longer than the bit anticipated for this pageant. I would recommend a mirror bit no longer than a minute. But find one or both of these on tape or DVD and watch them to learn how this bit can work.

Staging for a live performance requires that the performers stand at about a 45-degree angle to the audience, rather than with their shoulders perpendicular to the edge of the stage. With this angle, the face of one performer (preferably, the one playing Herod) will be visible to most of the audience, and the bodies of both performers will be more clearly visible. The easiest way to make sure the performers line up at a 45-degree angle is to put a strip of duct tape on the floor, and tell them, "That's where the mirror is."

When you watch the filmed versions of this bit, you'll notice right away that the second character is not following the first character's movements, but actually reflecting them as they occur. This requires tight choreography and timing. The best way to structure the bit is to begin with simpler effects:

★ Herod tries to clean the mirror, and Wise Person 3 follows suit, so their hands and rags touch.

Then you can end with more complicated ones:

★ Herod whips out a hat, and (surprise!) so does Wise Person 3; the hats don't match, but Herod doesn't notice.

And, of course, Wise Person 3 has to make a clean getaway when Herod is distracted by the Major Domo.

There are a few tricks you can use to have the performers start certain effects at the same time. Whichever side of the performers' bodies is farthest from the audience is their upstage side. For instance, if the performers are standing so that Herod's right shoulder is farthest from the audience and the Wise Person's left shoulder is farthest from the audience, then Herod's right and the Wise Person's left are their upstage sides. If Herod needs to start a move and cue the Wise Person to start with him, Herod can do this with a quick wink of his upstage eye, or by flicking the very tip of the tongue out of the upstage side of the mouth.

Don't use verbal cues, like a click of the teeth. It may be the audience is laughing so much that the performers can't hear each other.

You might think you need a wooden frame to show where the mirror is supposed to be to sell this to audience—you don't. The dialogue leading up to this establishes that Herod thinks there will be a mirror in the spot where they are performing. If the actors believe it's a mirror, then the audience will believe it's a mirror. If you have such a frame, and can set it up and take it down without unduly slowing down the pageant, fine; but it's not a necessity.

It took me four 1-hour rehearsals with Herod and Wise Person 3 to get the mirror bit down pat, which we did in the weeks before the rehearsals with the rest of the cast. The mirror bit *must* be performance-ready before you begin rehearsals with the entire cast. Working with Herod and Wise Person 3 on this for any length of time while the rest of the cast is standing around will defeat the purpose of splitting the cast for simultaneous rehearsals of the three acts.

Love Came Down at Christmas

WORDS: Christina G. Rossetti
MUSIC: Trad. Irish melody; transcribed by Allen Tuten
Transcription © 2006 Abingdon Press, admin. by The Copyright Co., Nashville, TN 37212

The Angel Spoke to Young Mary

WORDS: Trad. Cameroon
MUSIC: Trad. Cameroon, transcribed by John Bell; arrangement transcribed by Allen Tuten

It Came upon the Midnight Clear

WORDS: Edmund H. Sears
MUSIC: Richard S. Willis, transcribed by Allen Tuten
Transcription © 2006 Abingdon Press, admin. by The Copyright Co., Nashville, TN 37212

O Little Town of Bethlehem

WORDS: Phillips Brooks
MUSIC: Lewis H. Redner, transcribed by Allen Tuten

O Come, O Come, Emmanuel

WORDS: 9th cent. Latin
MUSIC: 15th cent. French, transcribed by Allen Tuten
Transcription © 2006 Abingdon Press, admin. by The Copyright Co., Nashville, TN 37212

Away in a Manger

WORDS: Anonymous
MUSIC: James R. Murray, transcribed by Allen Tuten
Transcription © 2006 Abingdon Press, admin. by The Copyright Co., Nashville, TN 37212

head.   The   stars   in   the   sky_____   looked
makes;   I   love   thee, Lord   Je - sus,   look
pray;   bless   all   the   dear   chil - dren   in

down   where   he   lay,   the   lit - tle   Lord
down   from   the   sky   and   stay   by   my
thy   ten - der   care,   and   fit   us   for

Je - sus,   a - sleep   on   the   hay.   2. The
cra - dle   till   morn - ing   is   nigh.   3. Be
heav - en   to   live   with   thee   there.

45

The First Noel

With feeling (♩ = 92)

1. The___ first___ No - el the___
(2. They)___ look - ed up, and___
(3. And___ by___ the_ light of___

an - gel did say was to cer - tain poor shep-herds in fields as they
saw___ a star shin-ing in___ the east___ be - yond___ them
that___ same star the___ Wise___ Men came___ from coun - try

lay; in___ fields___ where_ they lay_ keep - ing their sheep, on a
far; and_ to___ the___ earth it___ gave___ great light, and_
far; to___ seek___ for a king was_ their___ in - tent, and to

WORDS: Traditional English carol, alt.
MUSIC: Traditional English carol, transcribed by Allen Tuten
Transcription © 2006 Abingdon Press, admin. by The Copyright Co., Nashville, TN 37212

Joy to the World

WORDS: Isaac Watts
MUSIC: Arr. from G. F. Handel by Lowell Mason, transcribed by Allen Tuten
Transcription © 2006 Abingdon Press, admin. by The Copyright Co., Nashville, TN 37212

Love Came Down at Christmas (Reprise)

1. Love came down at Christ-mas, Love all love-ly,___ Love di-vine;___
2. Wor-ship we the God-head, Love in-car-nate,_ Love di-vine;___
3. Love shall be our to-ken; love be yours_ and_ love be mine;___

Love was born at Christ-mas; star and an-gels_ gave the sign.
wor-ship we our Je-sus, but where-with_ for_ sa-cred sign?
love to God and neigh-bor, love for plea_ and_ gift and sign.

WORDS: Christina G. Rossetti
MUSIC: Trad. Irish melody; transcribed by Allen Tuten
Transcription © 2006 Abingdon Press, admin. by The Copyright Co., Nashville, TN 37212

Notes

Notes

Notes

Notes

FaithSongs

Songs and Activities for Children Grades 2-6

FaithSongs is a collection of 125 songs for children in grades 2-6 and includes all of the teaching helps and ideas you need to teach and use music with children in choir, worship, Sunday school, and other settings.

• Songs included are from a wide variety of styles including traditional songs, praise and worship, children's anthems, new songs, and global song favorites.

• Create a core music system for your children's choir by using your denominational hymnal and *FaithSongs* together. Only *you* can choose the songs and anthems that will work best for the children in *your* church or Sunday school. Choir directors will discover ideas, tips, and teaching helps to enable them to introduce, teach, and sing each song. A reproducible children's choir rehearsal planning form is included in the Leader/Accompanist Edition.

• Wide range of uses in ministry with children!

❏ Use as a choir book. Enough songs for several years of use—a great investment!
❏ Use as a Sunday school songbook to engage the children as they develop their faith.
❏ Use to enhance the participation of the children in your worship services.

FaithSongs **includes songs to help children:**

• **Praise God!** Songs included for gathering and opening of worship, giving thanks and praise, proclaiming God's word, prayer, offering, Baptism, Communion, and sending forth.

• **Tell God's Story!** Songs include Bible story songs and songs to celebrate the Christian Year (Advent, Christmas and Epiphany, Lent, Easter and Eastertide, and Pentecost).

• **Celebrate God's Church!** Songs to help children as they discover the community of faith in celebration, music and singing, faith and trust, witness and service, and the community of God.

Several Editions Available!

The Leader/Accompanist Edition **(0687045797).** Includes full piano/vocal scores and guitar chords. Teaching hints and performance options are included for every song, as well as several indexes to help you choose music to fit your specific needs. Many songs also include sign language and movement activities. The performance options and teaching ideas were written by persons who are actively involved with children in church music. (Spiral)
$45.00

Singer's Edition **(068704569X).** Includes melody line and text for all songs. The sign language is also included in this edition to help reinforce your teaching. Use the Singer's Edition to help your children learn the text to the songs as well as to enhance the children's music skill learning. (Spiral)
$9.00

PLUS! *CD Split-Track Accompaniment Disk Set* **(0687046696).** This set of three CDs features split-track recordings of all the songs in *FaithSongs* for use as a listening/teaching tool and as accompaniment. Your children will love to sing with these cool tracks!
$45.00

Order from your favorite music dealer.

Abingdon Press

The Very Important Pageant CD Track List

#1. Overture: Love Came Down at Christmas

#2. Love Came Down at Chistmas*

#3. The Angel Spoke to Young Mary*

#4. It Came Upon the Midnight Clear*

#5. **SFX:** *Hotel Desk Bell*

#6. O Little Town of Bethlehem*

#7. O Come, O Come, Emmanuel*

#8. **SFX:** *Herald Trumpet*

#9. Away in a Manger*

#10. The First Noel*

#11. **SFX:** *Herald Trumpet*

#12. Joy to the World*

#13. Love Came Down at Christmas*

*Tracks 2, 3, 4, 6, 7, 9, 10, 12, and 13 are in split-track format.